Date: 11/24/21

J BIO FARMER
Chandler, Matt,
Declan Farmer : paralympic
hockey star /

Sports Illustrated KIDS

STARS OF SPORTS

DECLAN FARMER

PARALYMPIC HOCKEY STAR

by Matt Chandler

CAPSTONE PRESS
a capstone imprint

Stars of Sports is published by Capstone Press, an imprint of Capstone.
1710 Roe Crest Drive,
North Mankato, Minnesota 56003
www.capstonepub.com

SPORTS ILLUSTRATED KIDS is a trademark of ABG-SI LLC.
Used with permission.

**Library of Congress Cataloging-in-Publication data is available on the Library of
Congress website.**
ISBN: 978-1-4966-9530-7 (library binding)
ISBN: 978-1-9771-5409-5 (eBook PDF)

Summary: Provides an introduction to the life of Paralympic star Declan Farmer and
his career in sled hockey.

Editorial Credits
Editor: Mandy Robbins; Designer: Lori Bye; Media Researcher: Eric Gohl; Production
Specialist: Spencer Rosio

Image Credits
AP Images: Pavel Golovkin, 5, 15; Getty Images: Allen Berezovsky/WireImage, 19,
Buda Mendes, 22, Harry Engels, 14, 16, 17, Jason Connolly, 13, Martin Rose, 21;
Newscom: Eve Edelheit, 7, Mark Smith/ZUMA Press, 27, Mauro Ujetto, 23, Mike
Blake/REUTERS, 25, 28, ZUMA Press/Larry MacDougal, 11, ZUMA Press/Mark Reis,
Cover; Shutterstock: Adam Vilimek, 1; Sports Illustrated: David E. Klutho, 9

Direct Quotations
Page 6, from April 25, 2015, *USA Today* article "Declan Farmer to lead Team USA at
world championships," www.usatoday.com
Page 8, from March 8, 2018, Princeton Univeristy article "Going for gold, again: Declan
Farmer to compete in 2018 Paralympics", princeton.edu
Page 10,from April 25, 2015, *USA Today* article "Declan Farmer to lead Team USA at
world championships," www.usatoday.com
Page 26, from April 10, 2019, Team USA article "Sled Hockey Gold Medalist Declan
Farmer Refleccts on Growth of the Sport at Disabled Hockey Festival," teamusa.org

All internet sites appearing in back matter were available and accurate when this book
was sent to press.

TABLE OF CONTENTS

Glossary terms are **BOLD** on first use.

PRESIDENTIAL
HONORS

Imagine being a teenager and being honored by the president of the United States. Paralympic sled hockey champion Declan Farmer lived it. In 2014, Farmer led the United States Paralympic Sled Hockey Team to the gold medal. President Barack Obama invited the team to the White House to celebrate.

In his speech, the president honored Farmer for his play. The 16-year-old scored three goals and helped Team USA win the gold in back-to-back Paralympics.

Farmer called it "really cool" to be honored by the president. But it was just one of many thrilling moments in Farmer's career as one of the best sled hockey players of all time.

Farmer has faced a lifetime of challenges. Through it all, he has shown that, with hard work and determination, dreams can come true.

>>> Declan Farmer celebrates his goal against the Canadian team in the 2014 Winter Paralympics.

CHAPTER ONE

CHILDHOOD CHALLENGES

Declan Farmer was born in Tampa, Florida, on November 5, 1997. He was born with one of his legs missing above his knee. The other was missing below the knee. Farmer had to have six surgeries as a child. Soon, he was fitted with **prosthetic** legs.

Farmer's parents, Matt and Patti Farmer, didn't want his **disability** to slow him down. They got him involved in T-ball and soccer at a young age. In a 2015 interview, his father explained why competing in soccer became too hard for his son as he got older.

"The fields were small, so he could plant himself close to the goal, and he got plenty of goals that way," Matt Farmer told *USA Today*. "But once the fields got bigger, he couldn't get away with that."

Luckily for Farmer, he was about to discover a new sport—sled hockey.

》》》 Farmer (center) poses with a group
of extended family members after a
2014 high school pep rally.

Gear of the Game

The rules of sled hockey are very close to ice hockey. But
sled hockey players need some different equipment. They are
seated on metal sleds on blades. Instead of one long hockey
stick, a sled player has two short sticks. Each stick has metal
hooks called picks on the ends. The picks are used to dig into
the ice and pull the sled along. Sled hockey players must have
strong upper bodies to pull themselves up and down the ice.

COMPETITIVE HOCKEY

Farmer first tried sled hockey when he was eight years old. He fell in love with the sport right away.

"I couldn't get enough of it," Farmer said in 2018. "It was the first **adaptive sport** I had ever played. It was the first time I could really be competitive in something."

People who watched Farmer play said he was a natural. Sled hockey player Ron Richardson compared him to hockey superstar Wayne Gretzky.

"You could tell right away he had hockey sense," Richardson said.

Soon Farmer was playing in summer camps and youth clinics. He loved the game, but there were few chances to play sled hockey in Florida. That changed when the Tampa Bay Lightning of the National Hockey League (NHL) formed a sled hockey team. Farmer joined the team in 2007.

〉〉〉 Farmer grew up cheering on
the Tampa Bay Lightning. They
won the Stanley Cup in 2004.

FACT

Farmer's favorite NHL player is Steven
Stamkos. He plays for Farmer's hometown
team, the Tampa Bay Lightning.

CHAPTER TWO

INTERNATIONAL TEEN STAR

By the time he was 13, Farmer was a superstar on the ice. He continued to play for the Tampa Bay Lightning. In 2012, he earned a spot on the U.S. team competing at the World Sled Hockey Challenge in Alberta, Canada.

Though he was still in high school, Farmer was one of the best players in Alberta. He scored three goals and added three **assists** in the tournament. The United States beat Canada to win the gold medal! It was Farmer's first game against America's biggest hockey **rival**.

"On my first year on the team, everyone made it clear that we don't like Canada," he once said. "But we respect them, and the games are always very fun."

>>> Farmer (center) celebrates with his team after defeating Canada 1–0 at the World Sled Hockey Challenge Final.

The 2012 Challenge was the biggest win of Farmer's young career. It set the stage for future Paralympic glory!

FACT

In 2018, the World Sled Hockey Challenge changed its name to the Para Hockey Cup.

SILVER MEDALIST

In 2013, Farmer competed at the International Paralympic Committee (IPC) Ice **Sledge** Hockey World Championship.

Farmer scored two goals in the opening game between the United States and Sweden. The U.S. team won 7–0!

One of Farmer's most exciting goals came in the second game. The United States was taking on Norway. Midway through the first period, Farmer raced up the ice and caught a pass on a **breakaway**. The young star used his sled to move the puck. He raced toward the goal, passing the puck between his sticks.

With only the goalie between him and the goal, Farmer rocketed a wrist shot into the top-right corner of the net. He gave his team a 2–0 lead. The U.S. team won 7–0. With two more wins, they moved on to the gold-medal game.

>>> Farmer handles the puck while practicing with Team USA's 2014 Paralympic team.

The United States eventually lost to Canada in the finals. Still, Farmer delivered with four goals and four assists in the tournament.

FACT

Farmer eats a peanut butter and jelly sandwich in the locker room before every game.

CHAPTER THREE

PARALYMPIC STAR

Farmer was just 16 years old when he played in his first Paralympic Games. It was 2014, and he traveled to Sochi, Russia, to compete for Team USA. Farmer made an early difference in the games. He scored Team USA's first goal of the Paralympics. He added an assist in the 5–1 win over Italy.

〉〉〉 Russian player Dmitrii Lisov chases Farmer (right) down the ice in a match between Russia and Team USA in the 2014 Paralympics.

>>> Farmer handles the puck in the
semifinals against Canada in the 2014
Paralympics.

But it was once again Team Canada that brought
out the best in Farmer. This time, the two teams
met up in the semifinals. The Americans had just
lost to Russia. They needed a big game, and Farmer
delivered.

With just under six minutes left in the first period,
the game was scoreless. Farmer broke free in front
of the net and flipped a shot on goal. Canadian
goaltender Corbin Watson made the save. But it
bounced off his pad and slid into the net for the goal!

BEING THE BEST

Team USA added two more goals to win in a 3–0 shutout. Farmer helped to score all three goals in the game. He scored two and assisted on one.

Team USA earned a rematch against Russia in the gold-medal game. Though he didn't score, Farmer played well. He helped the United Stated earn a 1–0 win for the gold.

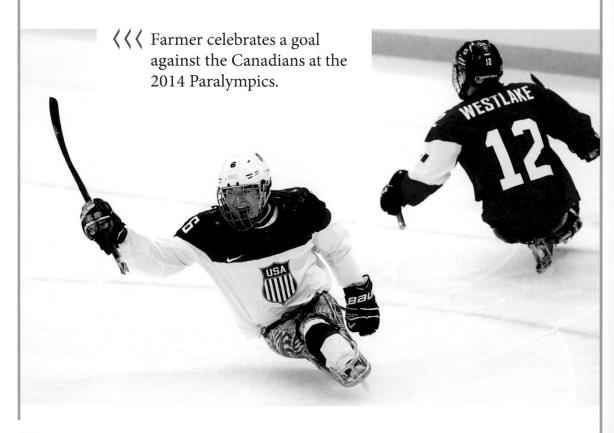

⟨⟨⟨ Farmer celebrates a goal against the Canadians at the 2014 Paralympics.

<<< Farmer (left), Brody Roybal (center), and Jen Lee (right) of Team USA celebrate their Paralympic gold medals.

Farmer led his team in scoring with three goals and five points during the Paralympics. He was named the Best Male Paralympic Athlete at the Sochi Paralympic Games. Best of all, he went home with the gold medal!

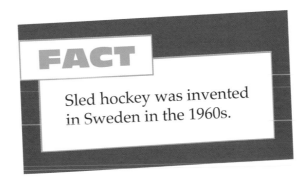

FACT

Sled hockey was invented in Sweden in the 1960s.

LIFE AFTER THE PARALYMPICS

In 2015, Farmer and Team USA returned to the World Championship in Buffalo, New York. Team USA had won the silver medal in 2013.

In five games, Farmer played great. He scored six goals—more than any other player on Team USA. He was named the Player of the Game in a 7–0 win over Italy. But, just like in the 2014 Paralympics, Farmer saved his best work for the gold-medal game against Canada.

Deep into the third period, the teams were tied at zero. Then Farmer stepped up. The 17-year-old took a pass in front of the Canadian goal. Farmer faked a high shot. Canadian goaltender Corbin Watson froze. Farmer quickly slid the puck into the bottom-right corner for the goal! The Americans went on to win the game 3–0 and earn the gold medal.

Farmer poses at the 2014 ESPY Awards. 〉〉〉

CHAPTER FOUR
RETURN TO GOLD

The 2018 Paralympic Games were held in PyeongChang, South Korea. The U.S. men's sled hockey team was hoping to win its third straight gold medal. Farmer came out strong and led the United States. He had nine goals and five assists in the first four games.

Many people, including head coach Guy Gosselin, were calling Farmer the best sled hockey player in the world. But Farmer wasn't satisfied with four great games. He wanted to win his second Paralympic gold.

If Team USA was going to win another gold, they had to beat Canada. The two teams faced off in the gold-medal game. Late in the third period, Canada led 1–0. It looked like Farmer and his teammates would have to settle for the silver medal.

Farmer controls the puck against the Korean $\rangle\rangle\rangle$
team in the 2018 Paralympics.

LEADING THE COMEBACK

With less than a minute left, the Canadian fans began to celebrate. That's when Farmer made the biggest play of the game. Teammate Brody Roybal raced down the left side of the ice. He passed the puck over the middle. It bounced off the stick of forward Kevin McKee and slid to Farmer. Farmer delivered a quick wrist shot past the goaltender. He tied the game with 37 seconds to go!

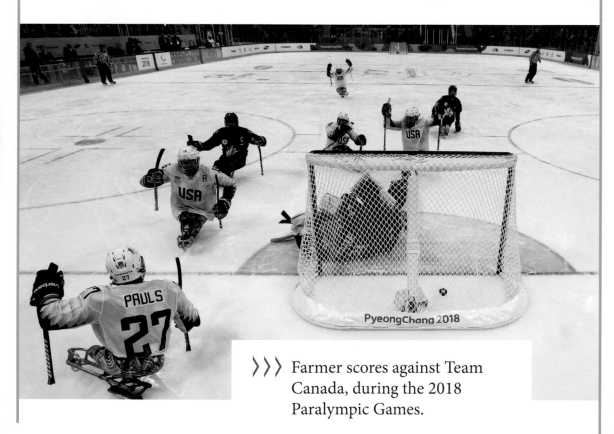

〉〉〉 Farmer scores against Team Canada, during the 2018 Paralympic Games.

Farmer and teammate Jack Wallace celebrate 〉〉〉
Farmer's goal against Team Canada during the
2018 Paralympic Games.

Less than four minutes into **overtime**, Farmer
struck again. He grabbed a rebound deep in Canada's
end. Farmer circled around and skated through three
defenders. He lined up and ripped a wrist shot into
the net. The Americans were gold-medal champions!

WORLD CHAMPIONSHIPS

Next up was a return to the World Sled Hockey Championships, now called the 2019 Para Ice Hockey World Championship. As usual, Team USA would have to play Canada in the gold-medal game. Over the course of the tournament, Farmer had seven goals and seven assists. It was impressive, but he saved his best work for the final game.

Canada led 2–1 late in the third period. Farmer brought his team back. With less than three minutes to go, he caught a loose puck. He quickly switched hands and beat Canadian goaltender Dominic Larocque to tie the game 2–2!

In overtime, Farmer found teammate Brody Roybal cutting down the left side toward Canada's goal. His perfect pass set up the game-winner. Farmer had led his team to the gold medal once again!

>>> Farmer poses for a portrait in his Team USA gear.

FACT

Farmer was named Player of the Game in the gold-medal game. He earned the title Best Forward of the Tournament at the 2019 World Championships.

CHAPTER FIVE
A BRIGHT FUTURE

Ask Declan Farmer about his plans after hockey, and he will tell you he isn't done playing. Even with all of his success, Farmer is still a young player.

"I love playing hockey and being part of a team," he says.

That love of the game will keep him training hard and competing on the ice. Farmer has listed capturing another gold medal as his top goal.

Still, there will be a time when Farmer **retires** from the game. He has already shown he is more than just a hockey player. Farmer earned a degree in economics from Princeton University in 2020. He is interested in coaching once his playing days are over. He already coaches at summer camps and clinics through the Tampa Bay Lighting. Fans hope Farmer may coach Team USA someday.

<<< Farmer speaks to a crowd at a 2017 Team USA event.

Equality for Athletes

The Paralympics are the third-biggest sporting event in the world. But until recently, the athletes were not treated the same as Olympic athletes. Olympic medalists received $37,500 for winning gold. When he won his first gold medal in 2014, Farmer and his teammates each received just $7,500. In 2018, the United States Olympic Committee changed the rules. Beginning in 2018, Farmer and all Paralympic athletes earned the same pay as Olympians.

Declan Farmer never let his disability stop him. He worked hard. He trained, and he never gave up on his dream. He is a gold-medal winner. He is a superstar of sled hockey. Farmer has worked hard off of the ice too. He has shown that a disability doesn't define who a person is. He became an international athlete. He was a successful college student. And he is an inspiration for people all over the world.

⟨⟨⟨ Farmer at the 2017 U.S. Olympic Committee Media Summit

TIMELINE

1997   Declan Farmer is born in Tampa, Florida, on November 5.

2013   Farmer competes in his first World Championship in Lyon, France. His team wins the silver medal.

2014   Farmer wins his first gold medal at the Paralympics in Sochi, Russia.

2015   Farmer wins the gold medal at the World Championship in Buffalo, New York.

2016   Farmer graduates from Berkeley Preparatory School.

2017   Farmer wins the silver medal at the World Championships in PyeongChang, South Korea.

2018   Farmer wins his second gold medal at the Paralympic Games in China.

2019   Farmer wins the gold medal at the World Championships in Ostrava, Czech Republic.

2020   Farmer graduates from Princeton University with a degree in economics.

GLOSSARY

ADAPTIVE SPORT (uh-DAPf-tiv SPORT)—sport where some of the rules are changed to allow players with disabilities to play

ASSIST (uh-SIST)—a pass that leads to a score by a teammate

BREAKAWAY (BRAYKE-uh-way)—when a player has the puck and there are no defenders between him and the goaltender

DISABILITY (dis-uh-BI-luh-tee)—something that restricts people in what they can do, usually because of an illness, injury, or condition present at birth

OVERTIME (OH-vur-time)—an extra period played if the score is tied at the end of a game

PROSTHETIC (pross-THET-ik)—an artificial part that takes the place of a body part, such as an arm or leg

RETIRE (ri-TIRE)—to give up a line of work

RIVAL (RYE-vuhl)—a person or group with whom you compete

SLEDGE (slej)—a term used outside of the United States to describe sled hockey

READ MORE

Chandler, Matt. *The Science of Hockey: The Top Ten Ways Science Affects the Game.* North Mankato, MN: Capstone Press, 2016.

Derr, Aaron. *Sports of the Paralympic Games.* Egremont, MA: Red Chair Press, 2020.

Herman, Gail. *What Are the Paralympic Games?* New York: Penguin Workshop, 2020.

INTERNET SITES

Declan's Story
choa.org/patients/patient-and-employee-stories/declan-farmer

U.S. Hockey Biography
teamusa.usahockey.com/page/show/3645486-declan-farmer

U.S. Paralympics Sled Hockey
teamusa.org/US-Paralympics/Sports/Sled-Hockey

INDEX